22/10/21.

To you and your beautiful daughter.

With love always,
Jaimie
xxx.

TINY LUNGS

25/6/21

DARLING GEORGI,

Your time may be limited,
but words are sweet, I hope
you enjoy these.
To you and your beautiful
daughter,
with love always,
Tatum's
Mum

TINY LUNGS

28 poems

Joanna Bennett
illustrations by arthur morgan aged 5

Copyright © 2020 Joanna Bennett

All rights reserved. This book or any portion thereof may not be reproduced or used in any manner whatsoever without the express written permission of the publisher except for the use of brief quotations in a book review.

First Printing, 2020

The Whole Gang Press
Bristol
www.thewholegangpress.co.uk

Words, design and layout by Joanna Bennett

www.tatterhood.co.uk
@tatterhood_

For Wesley, Arthur and Mabel

Contents

INHALATION

Bones	13
The Light On A Sequin	15
Fine	17
Replay / Rewind	19
Child	21
Love Notes To Europe	23
Sands	25
Dial Up	27
A T-Shirt With A Pocket	29
Lockdown 2020	31
Locked In / Locked Down	33
Home School	35
Lights Out	37
Hiraeth	39

EXHALATION

Book Worm	41
Tides	43
Firsts	45
Kernel	47
Slow Burner	49
Ballerina Music Box	51
The Sea	53
Fossils And Castles	55
Astronomer	57
For My Son, For My Daughter	59
Lifeblood	61
Tiny Lungs	63
Years End	65
Curtain Call	67

Acknowledgements

With thanks to Mum, Dad and Wesley for their unwavering support, love and kindness. Thank you for everything.

A huge thank you to Arthur for illustrating this book, you are a fantastic artist. Your drawings make us so happy.

And thank you for everything Arthur and Mabel. You are quite simply wonderful.

Introduction

Inhalation / Exhalation

In difficult times the inhalations are shallow, tense, tight, anxious, emphasised. The exhalations bring release, lowering the heart rate, releasing tension, breathing out any toxins and allowing fresh oxygen to flood back in.

The poems here take in the inhalations and exhalations of the last few years in my life, my oxygen, my carbon dioxide. The unexpected things, the different narratives, the dark rooms, the light rooms, the joy of the everyday, the loss of dear family members, the incredible children, the changing political landscapes, the giving birth and raising of children in a pandemic, the yearning for the loved ones we are desperate to see and the deep love, kindness and laughter I have gratitude for.

The inhalations and the exhalations sit side by side, companion ups and downs, intertwining at times. And I realise I am glad for the cycles that bring me to this point.

> Breathe in, breathe out. Tiny precious lungs.

Bones 🦴

Bones

Friend, let me sit beside you,
let me take those sorrow stones.
I'd like to ease the burden
that's been weighing down your bones.

We don't have to speak,
and I'll just keep them here with me.
So let your shoulders fall,
I'll take this watch and oversee.

And if you want them back
they are yours, save one or two.
We'll walk this path together,
and I will carry them for you.

The light on a sequin

The Light On A Sequin

I am the light on a sequin,
the swirl as you're stirring your tea.
I am the bit in that favourite song,
and toes running away from the sea.

I am the first flash of spring,
the warmth of the sun on your skin.
I am the mischief that catches your cheeks,
and the twinkling laughter within.

I am the love all around you,
the pattern, the colour, the form.
I am the voice that spurs you on,
the quiet and calm in the storm.

For Elizabeth x

Fine

Fine

Come into my arms and we'll remember.
We'll honour the hopes,
we'll think of the dreams,
and the times we dared to think.

Let the heavy,
let the hot,
and let the new tears fall.
For I will catch them each and all.

And together let us sit,
and know it will be fine.

For we will make it so.

Replay / Rewind

These are the small things, that if I don't collect,
I worry, in time, I might just forget.

An exact turn of phrase, hand reaching out for mine,
the characters and favourites all laid out in a line.

The finger that points to a tower in a book,
your hair wet, defiance, that laughter, a look.

I study you in moments, the quiet times, my muse,
curating the slide show, my rose-tinted views.

child ♥

Child

Every day I rise and wake,
my child walks beside me.
A peppered sky, a flash of song,
a whisper on a calm sea.

They skip along and brush my legs,
my child runs beside me.
Arms aloft I raise them high,
my dear child all around me.

At end of day, exhale replete,
my child lies beside me.
Aging now, they stay the same,
my child how I loved thee.

Love notes to Europe

Letter

Love Notes To Europe

A love letter to Paris,
a postcard sent from France,
the lifetimes full of wanderings,
and evenings filled with dance.

Sandy legs on beaches,
and waist belts made of sweets,
passports filled with ink spots,
hot smiling, unclosed streets.

Our hearts and minds propped open,
a welcome at our door,
a difference marked in name alone,
unbreakable rapport.

zands

Sands

And what to do with the grief, the knot,
the one it seems that time forgot.
To draw it in and hold it close?
Or breathe it out,
imbibe a dose?
Or feel the sands beneath your toes,
and press the pulse before it goes.
Lids look upon a distant shore,
exhale until it's gone once more.

Dial up

Dial Up

I don't want
to touch base,
to reach out,
to loop back,
and conversate.

I don't want
to watch this space,
to pass it on,
to get my ducks all in a row.

I guess I want the human touch,
a warm eye meeting mine.
A voice to say,
"It's cold outside."
And then,
"So how are you?"

And then a pause, enough to think,
enough for me to say,
"The sun it broke a bit today."
And, "Yeah, I think okay."

A T-shirt with a pocket

A T-Shirt With A Pocket

A young man at sea, a photo in a wallet,
a packet, then a comb, a t-shirt with a pocket.

A western playing low and a paper on the side,
A Rich Tea and a coaster, deep devotion for a bride.

A twinkle and a smile as his wellies walked ahead,
"Just don't get old." my grandfather said.

A life well lived, the laughter in a room,
a star on the field and a garden so in bloom.

And we raise our tankards high, and slip half a crown,
'cos we'll never let the bastards grind us down.

Lockdown 2020

Stepping aside, access denied,
trying to do the right thing.

Children at home, a solitary roam,
a pendulum losing it's swing.

Face covered in pen, recycled card den,
a rainbow is chalked onto stone.

A call made at dawn, a baby is born,
a family meets on the phone.

A grandparent waits, to reopen the gates,
a thousand hugs in the bank.

As beloved ones fall, our part is just small,
and an army of people to thank.

Earth

Looner moom

Locked In / Locked Down

I don't really know why we don't say it by phone,
because I know we've been blue on our own.
I suppose we try to be brave for the other,
so we text and chit-chat of paint colour.

We talk of our lunch, and "Hey, how's the garden?",
how the government's run by these fools.
We chew the fat, unkempt hair and that,
and when maybe they'll open the schools.

But he says, "Look at this, a collage I made,
our memories from over the years."
There's driftwood from France,
a stone plucked by chance,
I feel the bittersweet tears.

So if I don't say it, I will write it here,
I miss you, it's been really hard.
I can't wait to see you, and next year we'll hug,
and I'll run over to hand you my card.

Home School

A school at home, just you and us,
our makeshift, hopeful syllabus.
I'm not sure that we taught you much,
half-naked work call zooms and such.

At first we tried some maths, the phonics,
avoiding pre-lunch gin and tonics.
Crafts and paints, a primary hue,
how to turn the air a shade of blue.

And you became a fine big brother,
teaching us selfless love for another.
You told of atoms, skies and rockets,
drawings spilled from walls and pockets.

And I can see you taught us well,
as we laughed and cried and tried to spell.
I pack your lunch through misty glasses,
I'll be signing up for your evening classes.

Lights Out

Lights Out

I've watched you sleep a thousand times,
I'm sorry I haven't as much of late.
Beautiful boy, eyes closed, divine,
You'd never let on you've had to wait.

hiraeth

Hiraeth

Each day at six, eyes searching the ceiling,
I get this malaise, a fleeting feeling.

I speak with myself, "It'll pass by quick."
And I realise then, it's like I'm homesick.

It's not for a place or a certain time,
More a yearn for what was, a midnight chime.

I long to return to a certain land,
A place where it's warm, where I can hold a hand.

A place where my father can hold my baby,
Somewhere soon, eyes closed, maybe.

Book worm

Book Worm

Close your eyes and dive
into the pages of a book.

Swim, swim down
into the warm, the fuzz, the nook.

The old, the new, the well-thumbed tome,
the break, the slip, your place, a home.

The freedom that comes from reading the words,
in the smallest rooms, the soaring birds.

The greatest gift you'll ever share,
your ticket to ride to anywhere.

Tides ΛΛΛΛΛΛ

Tides

I draw a path, a circle, a line,
enclosing my loves, my family, mine.
I keep them as close as I can for a while,
before we swim off in more singular file.

I want to revel and rejoice in our bubble,
as we weightlessly float,
upstream from the muddle.

I prepare for the change and the shift in the tide,
when it may not be nature to swim by my side.
But this is a constant, your haven, our sea,
a refuge, safe waters, for you and for me.

FIRSTS.

Firsts

And so, with that, you're in through the door,
your bag on a hook with a name.

And I can't quite believe that we're here,
that it's come,
but my goodness I'm glad that I came.

Kernel

Kernel

Your essence, she said, is inside like a kernel,
soft, safe from harm, full of hope, vernal.

Despite outside forces, the daily grind, a toasting,
it can endure a lot, a wise crack, a roasting.

A pulse, a heart, it keeps on glowing,
cheering you on, the roar keeps growing.

So when it's very dark, listen hard, use your gut,
you're stronger than you know,
keep going little nut.

slow burner

Slow Burner

My baby marvels at the lines upon my face,
They trace a line, velvet terrain, crossing narrative and pace.

She takes her time to kneel before the skin beneath her hands,
Delighting in the landscape of these softly yielding lands.

To her she sees the merit in the well read creased slow burner,
The well-worn page, the lived in cover,
the well-beloved page turner.

Her smiling eyes will scold of how we rate ourselves and fret,
Shaking head at our cold tones and the misty eyed regret.

To her she sees the wonder, not a list of things undone,
A seasoned frequent flyer, 43 times round the sun.

Ballerina music
BOX

♪♫♩

Ballerina Music Box

A slowly opened box lighting up a wide-eyed face,
the dancing girl within, moves with porcelain edged grace.
A glint about her eye and some mischief in her smile,
she relishes the chance to freely dance a little while.

And as the years unfold, other faces join the girl,
they too marvel at her poise, the life, the blood, the whirl.
The motor pushes on, but the lines are proudly won,
the colours and the fabrics gently worn by the sun.

The music may be slowing now, still spinning tiny feet,
she dances on her own card now and she curates the beat.
The key tightens up with age, but the melody plays on,
ballerina dancing, she still cherishes the song.

The

Sea

The Sea

He visits the shore day in, day out,
countless times he has looked upon this blue.
It knows his joys, his sadness, his secrets, his truth,
the story of each line etched in his skin.
He stays until the night draws in,
when the sands cool and the sun moves on.
He looks upon the water, out to the rolling sea,
and nods with gratitude as he turns to leave.

fossils and castles

Fossils And Castles

He's fossils and castles and pools on a beach,
with strong arms and steady hands always in reach.

Two girls run in circles and mirror his stride,
legs tripping together, comrades side by side.

He's stories and campfires, a life shining bright,
a love for a woman burning in the starlight.

A teacher encouraging others to grow,
he listens and watches the ebb and the flow.

The boy in the valleys, a star since arrival,
our ultimate hero, put simply our idol.

Astronomer

Astronomer

Milky dark and violet blue,
a ceiling sky to wander through.

A globe to spin, untapped potential,
my love for you is elemental.

FOR MY SON.
FOR MY DAUGHTER

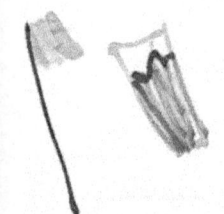

For My Son, For My Daughter

A letter to my son, a letter to my daughter,
please brush your teeth and drink lots of water.

Yes do evolve, but also never change,
keep hold of the colour, the warmth, the strange.

It's easy to lose hours staring out of the window,
daydreaming is good, but remember to stop, continue.

Gratitude and space will serve you well,
read people's faces and hear the stories they tell.

Please take the time to sit with my mother,
she'd love to hear your news, the good, the other.

People will hurt you, but make it your power,
harness the good, observe and flower.

Capture the small things, the smell, the taste, the touch,
and I will try too,

(I love you so much.)

life BIOOd

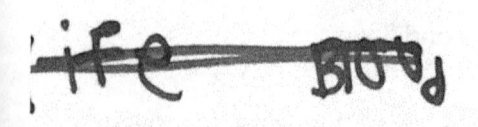

Lifeblood

Most ferocious beating heart,
my love is written deep.

Symbiotic, side by side,
child I miss you when you sleep.

Tiny Lungs

Tiny Lungs

I like to listen to you breathe in the dark.
Squinting, eyes level to see your chest rise and fall,
rise and fall,
rise and fall,
tiny lungs.
I rest a hand on the warm skin to feel the in and out,
the out and in.
Every night I do the same with your brother,
an eye across his broadening chest watching the breath
rise and fall, fall and rise.
I marvel at the thought of the tiny lungs beneath your skin,
inhaling and exhaling, inhaling, exhaling.
I imagine the places you will visit,
the air that will fill your lungs.
Those lungs of yours and your brother.
The hot and the sticky, too thick to take in,
the cold and the quick taking your breath away.
I hope to watch you and to breathe it too, side by side for a good while.
Slowly rise and slowly fall.

years end

Year's End

And if you choose to reminisce,
to recollect a lover's kiss,
or softly rise to share a verse,
or write a thought, or brew a curse.
Think his is his and yours is yours,
the sun will set and rise of course.
The noise you hear, well that's the clock,
a smiling face, companion tock.
A chapter's end, the closing scenes,
the streamers, cads, the beauty queens.
But take a bow, however low,
they're standing up, so on we go.

Curtain Call

And looking at it all, the autumn, summer, spring,
would I alter any parts? Would I change a single thing?

No, I'd replay all the dancing, the cast in fullest song,
the movie scenes, the in-betweens, the laughter ever strong.

I'd remember those young hearts emblazoning the night,
the bodies making stories and the fires burning bright.

I'd look toward my sweetheart, take their hand in mine,
and say with fiercest love, "I had a damn good time."

Index

A

A T-Shirt With A Pocket. 29
Astronomer. 57

B

Ballerina Music Box. 51
Bones. 13
Book Worm. 41

C

Child. 21
Curtain Call. 67

D

Dial Up. 27

F

Fine. 17
Firsts. 45
For My Son, For My Daughter. 59
Fossils And Castles. 55

H

Hiraeth. 39
Home School. 35

K

Kernel. 47

L

Lifeblood. 61
Lights Out. 37
Lockdown 2020. 31
Locked In / Locked Down. 33
Love Notes To Europe. 23

R

Replay / Rewind. 19

S

Sands. 25
Slow Burner. 49

T

The Light On A Sequin. 15
The Sea. 53
Tides. 43
Tiny Lungs. 63

Y

Years End. 65

About The Author

Joanna was longlisted for the Out-Spoken Prize For Poetry in 2017. Her debut poetry book Swimming Underwater was published in 2017. In December 2017 she was commissioned by GOSH Arts to write a book for Great Ormond Street Hospital in collaboration with illustrator Sarah Dennis. It was subsequently turned into a film read by Rupert Everett. She has had poems featured in numerous magazines. She lives in Bristol with her partner and two young children.

www.tatterhood.co.uk
@tatterhood_

Lightning Source UK Ltd.
Milton Keynes UK
UKHW020740180521
383915UK00006B/238